HR's Contribution to International Mergers and Acquisitions

Chris Rees
Tony Edwards

The Chartered Institute of Personnel and Development is the leading publisher of
books and reports for personnel and training professionals, students, and all those
concerned with the effective management and development of people at work.
For full details of all our titles, please contact the Publishing Department:

Tel: 020 8263 3387
Fax: 020 8263 3850
E-mail: publish@cipd.co.uk

To view and purchase the full range of CIPD publications:
www.cipd.co.uk/bookstore

HR's Contribution to International Mergers and Acquisitions

Chris Rees
Kingston University

Tony Edwards
King's College London

© Chartered Institute of Personnel and Development 2003

All rights reserved. No part of this publication may be reproduced, stored in an information storage and retrieval system, or transmitted in any form or by any means, electronic, mechanical, photocopying, recording or otherwise without the written permission of the Chartered Institute of Personnel and Development, CIPD House, Camp Road, London SW19 4UX

First published 2003

Cover design by Curve
Designed and typeset by Beacon GDT
Printed in Great Britain by Short Run Press

British Library Cataloguing in Publication Data
A catalogue record for this book is available from the British Library

ISBN 1 84398 031 2

Chartered Institute of Personnel and Development
CIPD House, Camp Road, London SW19 4UX

Tel: 020 8971 9000
Fax: 020 8263 3333
Website: www.cipd.co.uk

Incorporated by Royal Charter: Registered charity no. 1079797.

Contents

Acknowledgements		vi
Executive summary		vii
Chapter 1	Introduction	1
Chapter 2	Globalisation, national effects and international M&As: context, issues and methods	5
Chapter 3	Home country effects: company nationality in merging companies and the impact on HR	9
Chapter 4	Host country effects: comparing a merged company's HR practices in different countries	13
Chapter 5	Organisational structures and cultures: the impact of mixed heritage in mergers	19
Chapter 6	The process and politics of mergers: timing, resistance and compromise	25
Chapter 7	The HR role in mergers: key policy areas and the lessons learned	31
Chapter 8	Conclusions for management Richard L Coates	39
References		44

Acknowledgements

The CIPD would like to thank the authors Tony Edwards and Chris Rees, for researching and writing this excellent Research Report.

Thanks also go to the CIPD's co-sponsors of the research, Mercer Human Resource Consulting and PricewaterhouseCoopers (PwC) and to members of the Steering Group who have guided this research project through its various stages. Steering group members are Andrea Arnold at PwC, Richard Coates at Mercer Human Resource Consulting, Nickie Fonda at the CIPD, Richard Greenhill, an independent remuneration and HR adviser, Marc Hommel at PwC and Frances Wilson at the CIPD.

We are very appreciative of members of the CIPD's International Forum and the people who were interviewed for the case studies for contributing their time and expertise to this research.

Frances Wilson
Manager, International, CIPD

John Campbell
Vice President, International, CIPD

Executive Summary

It is well established that mergers and acquisitions (M&As) are fraught with difficulties, many of which relate to HR issues. International M&As are even more problematical. When engaging in cross-border deals or acquiring an organisation with operations in many countries, legislative frameworks, ways of doing business and cultural differences will all provide hurdles not found to the same extent in single-country deals. The report considers both the home-country and host-country effects on international M&As through a series of in-depth case studies.

These case studies demonstrate that the nationality (home) of the acquirer makes a significant difference to the style and culture of the new organisation, as well as to the ways in which the merger process itself unfolds. Likewise national (host) differences in patterns of HRM and industrial relations also inform the way that post-merger integration takes place across countries, with marked differences evident in many respects. Moreover, the case studies highlight how that process is an intensely political one, involving a series of negotiations and compromises as key players seek ways of achieving balance in the new organisation.

The report identifies and discusses particular areas of HR policy that are central to the successful handling of international M&As, in particular:

- pay and benefits
- management selection and development
- harmonisation and integration
- employee communication
- the pace of change.

The report also assesses the factors that determine the level of influence HR is able to have in international M&As, and draws out the main lessons for HR managers. There is a range of key issues that HR needs to address if the chances of success are to be optimised. These include:

- understanding, prior to embarking on acquisition, the strategic rationale underpinning the deal, together with the external constraints

- ensuring that cultural due diligence is carried out prior to a deal, so that effective integration programmes can be implemented immediately post-deal

- moving quickly but fairly in the appointment of new management teams at all levels in the business, and dealing humanely with the casualties

- identifying realistic synergy targets, and exercising caution in estimating both the timeframe and the potential cost of redundancies

- ensuring that due diligence provides comprehensive data on all aspects of reward, and that the costs of harmonisation or pragmatism are factored into the deal

- establishing early a flexible project management process, and ensuring that it has the necessary resources.

The critical issues that undermine the success of mergers are frequently people-related. To this extent the report confirms what previous research has also highlighted. As such it is crucial that HR has a leading role to play. The report concludes that HR must be integral to the M&A process from the outset. To achieve this, the function must be a credible business-partner and generate practical, financially astute and timely solutions.

1 | Introduction

The problematic post-merger period at Corus

In June 1999 British Steel and the Dutch firm Hoogovens announced a cross-border merger worth nearly £4 billion. The deal took place within the context of a merger boom, and was justified on the basis that: (i) the scale of the new company would allow it to compete more effectively in an increasingly concentrated sector, and (ii) the scope for closures and rationalisations would reduce costs. At the time of the merger the prospects for the firm appeared to be bright, with management announcing a special dividend to shareholders and plans to realise cost savings of £194 million a year.

However, Corus has struggled to cope with adverse trading conditions and has been forced into a series of measures not envisaged at the time of the merger, involving unexpectedly deep cuts in employment. These failed to stem the group's losses, and in 2002 senior management came up with a proposal to pay off some of the company's ballooning debt. This involved a move away from its multi-metal strategy, announced at the time of the merger, by selling its aluminium division to Pechiney of France.

This proposal provoked serious internal ructions within the company. Many in the Dutch part of the firm were resentful, since it was here that the aluminium business was disproportionately located. In particular, some argued that the proceeds from the sale should be reinvested in the Netherlands rather than used to pay off the group's debt. There were wider reports of cultural divides between the Dutch and British parts of the company, and in early 2003 these reached a head when the Dutch supervisory board used its legal powers to block the sale. With the company's share price trading at a fraction of its value at the time of the merger, senior management embarked on yet another bout of cost-cutting at its British sites.

The rationale for the study

Corus is but one example of many companies that have faced problems following international mergers and acquisitions (M&As). While merged firms only rarely come to the point of bankruptcy, it is certainly a cautionary tale. Financial performance in firms formed through an international merger, generally, has failed to live up to expectations, and *people issues* are often cited as an explanatory factor (Mercer HR Consulting, 2002). One recent survey of multinational companies (MNCs) that had conducted an acquisition in the previous two years found that 87 per cent identified addressing short-term employee concerns as the single most important factor in ensuring the acquisitions met their business objectives (PwC, 2002).

Not surprisingly, this pattern of poor performance has given rise to a raft of publications on this issue. Some of these studies promise to provide a set of prescriptions that can be used in all types of international M&As and help to ensure that the merger is successful. One high-profile example is the book *Managing Human Resources in Cross-Border Alliances* by Randall Schuler *et al*. This offers a range of *guidelines* for human resource (HR) professionals who are engaged in international M&As. In one respect this approach has much to commend it; many firms and individuals are experiencing a merger with an international dimension for the first time, and the possible pitfalls are obvious from the Corus case.

> 'One recent survey of multinational companies ... found that 87 per cent identified addressing short-term employee concerns as the single most important factor in ensuring the acquisitions met their business objectives ... '

However, in this study we have sought to move beyond this kind of *blueprint* approach to change. By examining the processes involved in a number of international M&As, we were able to reveal the complexities of the post-merger period, showing variations between firms. We look to avoid the danger of making universal prescriptions or ones that are not informed by evidence. Accordingly, the report is based on a programme of case studies of firms engaged in international M&As, which provides a strong empirical base. We avoid the tendency among much of the literature to base claims on the views of one senior management respondent, using our in-depth case-study work at multiple levels to reveal a fuller picture. The approach is primarily analytical in that we undertake a detailed examination of the variety of processes we observed. We do not promise a range of prescriptions that are universally applicable; rather, we aim to stimulate the thoughts of HR practitioners concerning how they might handle the particular challenges they face in the specific context of their organisation.

Details of the study

Anecdotal evidence has suggested that there is a widespread concern among HR professionals about the way that HR issues are handled in international M&As. It was against this background that in 1999, the CIPD conducted a survey of its International Forum members, in order to gauge the opinion of senior HR people across a range of issues related to the process and outcomes of M&A activity. The results of this survey were published by the CIPD in 2000, in a survey report called *People Implications of Mergers and Acquisitions, Joint Ventures and Divestments*.

Following this survey, a further study was commissioned to look in far more depth at particular cases, and to track the process of merger activity over time. It is the findings from this more in-depth study that are reported here. The research was conducted and the report written jointly by Chris Rees (Kingston University) and Tony Edwards (King's College London).[1] The project was co-sponsored by the CIPD, Mercer Human Resource Consulting and PricewaterhouseCoopers.

The data are mainly qualitative, and the collection of data has been split into two phases. The first phase involved interviews at 12 organisations across six sectors (and has included some joint ventures, as well as acquisitions of different sizes and from different countries). A summary of the main findings from this first phase was published in *People Management* in 2002 ('Twin Piques', vol. 8, No. 12, 13 June 2002. pp 38–39). The second phase of the project examined four of these companies in more depth. Though reference is made in this report to some of the initial 12 companies, the bulk of the material is drawn from the four major cases. These four companies have been anonymised through the use of pseudonyms.

The major aim of the research was to address the issue of how the HR function can play a more consistent and more strategic role during, and particularly after, the merger process. A range of questions, some broad and some more particular, were considered:

- What role does the nationality of the parent firm have in the handling of HR issues?

> '… we aim to stimulate the thoughts of HR practitioners concerning how they might handle the particular challenges they face … '

◘ To what extent do national systems of regulation result in the M&A process occurring differently across countries?

◘ How do merged firms with a mixed heritage evolve in the post-merger period?

◘ How can we characterise the political dynamics and internal processes within merging companies?

◘ What are the key challenges for the HR function in international M&As?

◘ What lessons can be learned from the case studies for HR professionals and managers?

In compiling the report we have aimed to set the findings in a broader context, as well as capture as much of the illustrative detail from each case as we can. Hence the structure of the report moves from the broad issues of international restructuring and company nationality, through a consideration of organisational structures and cultures, and on to the specific area of HR interventions and influence.

Endnotes

1 Some additional fieldwork was conducted by Luis Ortiz (Universitat Pompeu Fabra, Barcelona), Xavier Coller (Universitat de Barcelona) and Michael Worttmann (Wissenschaftzentrum Berlin).

2 | Globalisation, national effects and international M&As: context, issues and methods

The aims of the study

Mergers and acquisitions are highly cyclical. The most recent cycle, which ran from the early 1990s to 2000, was distinguished not only by the record-breaking value and volume of M&As but also by the high proportion of international deals. Estimates suggest that 25 per cent of all M&As are cross-border in nature in that they involve firms from different countries joining together. In addition to this, there is an international element to many more mergers involving firms registered in the same country where one or both have operations in other countries.

Therefore, M&As are a key part of the process of the globalisation of the firm. Some observers have argued that international mergers are creating firms that no longer have a clear national home since they are organised to serve global markets and are not concentrated in, or reliant upon, any one country. From this perspective, the M&A process in general and the handling of HR issues in particular are shaped by global rather than national effects. An alternative view is that firms retain a strong national character, even when they acquire other firms internationally. The implication of this is that the nationality of the parent firm is influential in shaping the way that the merger process occurs, and in the way that HR issues are managed. The first issue that this report tackles is the extent to which there are particular *national effects from the parent firm* in international M&As.

A related issue is the role of national effects in shaping the way that M&As occur and evolve across borders. Have national cultures and forms of regulation become less important in the face of globalisation and the growth of MNCs? If so, we would expect there to be convergence in the way that HR issues are handled in merged firms. Or do cultures and regulations remain highly important, acting as major constraints on the behaviour of firms? If this were the case, we would expect to see merged firms adopting a quite different approach across borders. Thus the second issue the report gets to grips with is the role of the *national effects of host systems* in influencing the post-merger period.

A further related issue concerns cases where firms join forces in a deal billed as a *merger of equals*. While most mergers occur with one firm clearly in charge, a significant number of M&As in the most recent merger wave involved firms of roughly equal size. A series of questions arise from the mixed heritage in such companies. For example does the merged firm resemble a hybrid of both of the firms prior to the merger, or does one of the firms gradually emerge as the model on which the merged company is based? The report's third aim is to shed light on the influence of mixed heritage on the merger process.

The way in which merged firms evolve towards a hybrid of the two firms or become based clearly on one, raises questions concerning the way in which decisions on these issues are reached. Some writers on HR in international M&As imply that these decisions are the outcome of an ordered, rational process of assessing what each firm offers, with evaluations being made against objective criteria. Is this the way that decisions on HR issues are handled in the post-merger period? Or is this period one in which disagreements are rife, individuals and groups seek to advance or defend their own interests, and compromises have to be reached? Examining the politics of international M&As is the fourth aim of the report.

> 'The rationale for this was to gather a snapshot of a range of different types of international deals ... in a variety of sectors.'

The handling of particular HR issues should be seen in the light of these national and political factors. The strength of national effects, both from the parent firm and from the host business systems are likely to vary from one area of HR to another. Similarly, changes to some HR policies are likely to be much more sensitive, and therefore create more resistance, than changes to others. Are we able to sketch general tendencies between the ways that different HR issues are handled in international M&As? Answering this question is the fifth aim of the report.

A final set of issues relates to the role of the HR function in international M&As. Are HR professionals *strategic partners* in such mergers, tied in with top management and instrumental in the pre- and post-merger periods? Or are they marginalised, becoming involved at a relatively late stage, once key strategic decisions have been taken, and left to pick up the pieces? More generally, what lessons can be learned from the research concerning the role of HR during international M&As? This is the sixth and final objective of the report.

The methodology

The study on which this report is based was split into two phases. The first of these involved 12 firms in six different sectors: finance, IT, food, pharmaceuticals, utilities and oil. The rationale for this was to gather a snapshot of a range of different types of international deals – mergers of equals, acquisitions involving different nationalities of parent firm and joint ventures – in a variety of sectors. This phase involved the researchers interviewing one or a small number of people across these organisations. The details of these companies are displayed in Table 1.

Table | The firms involved in phase 1

Name	Sector	Details of the M&A
BritBank	Finance	A British bank acquiring banks in other countries
Global FinServices	Finance	An American financial services group involved in joint ventures in Europe
IT Services	IT/telecoms	An American group providing IT services on an outsourcing basis
TeleCo	IT/telecoms	A partly American-owned specialist IT and telecoms player
BritOil	Oil	A British oil major involved in a number of acquisitions
EuroFuel	Oil	A French oil major, created through two successive mergers
GlobalDrug	Pharmaceuticals	A major drugs firm created through the merger of a British and an Anglo-American firm
USPharma	Pharmaceuticals	An American drugs giant that acquired a smaller American firm
UKPower	Utilities	A British group involved in a number of acquisitions in Europe and North America
International Services	Utilities	A diversified French firm involved in a range of services, acquiring a series of small UK firms
SnackCo	Food	An American-owned firm acquiring a British-based provider of convenience foods
FastFood	Food	A major American provider of fast food that acquired a small British niche firm

> 'The data were primarily drawn from HR professionals, ... but we also interviewed a range of people from other functions ...'

The second and principal phase was to carry out more in-depth studies of a sub-set of these firms. These were selected to enable us to address the six research issues identified above. The four companies were:

- *SnackCo* – a division of a British multinational that was sold to an American company. The division has operations across a number of countries, significantly expanding the scope of the American parent. HR directors at European and British levels were interviewed and we were able to access a survey of employee views of the acquisition covering the UK and Spain.

- *BritOil* – a British oil firm that has engaged in a number of large acquisitions over the past few years. We examined one of these, the purchase of a specialist firm that was also British-owned, but highly spread across the world. We interviewed senior HR staff covering a number of regions, including the UK and Spain.

- *EuroFuel* – a French oil firm that has also been involved in a number of acquisitions, including one in Belgium and another with a former fierce rival in France. In this company we were able to interview a range of HR staff in the UK, France and Germany.

- *GlobalDrug* – a merger of equals between a British and an Anglo-American firm creating a large internationally spread firm with strong roots in both the UK and USA. The opportunity arose to carry out research in a number of countries where this firm had bases, and we interviewed extensively at HQ and at four comparable sites in the UK, USA, Germany and Spain, supplementing this with an interview in China.

In total, 64 interviews were conducted over an 18-month period, giving us a substantial body of data. Moreover, the diversity of the companies enabled us to address a range of research questions. The data were primarily drawn from HR professionals, allowing us to chart in detail the handling of HR issues, but we also interviewed a range of people from other functions, particularly in GlobalDrug. This allowed us to see the role of HR from a broader perspective, to investigate the way that formal policies are operated in practice, and to examine the handling of many issues that have HR consequences, but are not governed primarily by the HR function, such as decisions on where cuts in employment were to fall.

The data provide an excellent basis on which to shed light on a series of important questions. While the value and volume of international M&As have fallen back in the last three years, history tells us that their cyclical nature means that there will be another sharp rise at some stage. Reflecting on the way that many HR issues were handled in M&As that took place at the peak of the last boom, therefore, would appear to be particularly timely.

3 | Home country effects: company nationality in merging companies and the impact on HR

Sources of a 'home country effect'

One particularly important influence on merger activity is the way that the processes and outcomes of M&As are affected by the nationality of the parent firm, the so-called *home country effect*. There are a number of sources of evidence that indicate that the approach of MNCs to international human resource management (HRM) is strongly shaped by their ties to the country in which they originated. There are a range of reasons for this: MNCs tend to raise finance and have their shares traded primarily in their home country, and so are answerable to domestic banks and shareholders; the management boards of even highly internationalised firms are staffed disproportionately by nationals of the country of origin; and the culture of this country permeates the assumptions underlying a range of strategic and operational decisions whether the decision-makers realise this to be the case or not.

Therefore, we might expect the home country effect to be important in shaping the way that acquiring firms seek to manage and integrate those that they acquire. This is consistent with previous evidence that MNCs of different nationalities behave in nationally distinct ways in international M&As. For instance, Faulkner *et al* (2002: 120) found that 'significantly differing HRM policies are adopted by firms of different nationalities as they attempt to integrate and manage UK-acquired subsidiaries'. We are able to expand on these findings with reference to our qualitative data.

A distinct American influence

The first phase of the research project enabled us to consider a range of home country effects. The prevalence of American firms in the sample – seven of the 12 M&As had some American involvement – reflects the number of US MNCs that are engaged in acquisitions in Britain. While there was some diversity across these seven cases, there were also some common tendencies:

- the relatively centralised approach to making decisions on HR issues

- the moves to integrate quickly and sometimes aggressively in the search for cost savings

- the strong desire to link pay to performance in acquired units.

These tendencies show up in four particular case studies. First, in Global FinServices (a financial services group), we examined the role of the American parent firm in managing its joint ventures in Europe. It was evident that the company has a range of international HR policies in its fully owned operations, governing issues such as appraisal and compensation. This was to some extent carried over into its joint ventures; in both of the main cases described to us, Global FinServices had taken a much more active role in managing HR than its partner firm, exerting an influence over issues like pensions, which are not covered by Transfer of Undertakings regulations, and instigating moves to establish a clear sense of identity within the joint venture.

> '... acquisitions involving an American firm often led to a clear and distinct influence over the way that HR issues are handled.'

At SnackCo, one of the main case studies, the influence of the American parent is also clear. The acquired division had been used to operating more or less autonomously from its British parent, but under American ownership there was an increased need to justify deviations from a global corporate approach in areas like pay for performance. At a European level, those in the HR function put great emphasis on the financial costs of not being compliant: as one interview respondent put it, 'Show an American the financial risk of not doing it the required way and they ... understand that language.'

In both pharmaceuticals companies (see Table 1) a distinctively American approach is also evident. In USPharma, the rapid speed of integration between sales teams was notable with the American parent making it clear that it expected this to be the case. In GlobalDrug, similarly, the influence of the American party to the merger was clearly evident. The merger brought together a British firm that had tended to operate on a decentralised basis – 'It was like having an absentee parent', as one American respondent put it – with a much more centralised Anglo-American firm. It was evident that the latter firm was serving as the model for the newly merged company, adopting a much more centralised approach in pushing particular policies from America, such as the pay/performance link and the use of contingent workers.

In short, acquisitions involving an American firm often led to a clear and distinct influence over the way that HR issues are handled. On occasions, the British managers in our case-study firms argued that this was problematic, because of the ignorance of the nature of regulations in many European countries and the great differences between these countries. How does the American influence compare with those M&As involving firms of other nationalities?

Comparing British and French influences

We can contrast the American firms with those of French and British origins. In one French firm in the utilities sector – International Services – the evidence pointed to a quite different approach. Our contact in this firm described the acquisition of an American firm and the clashes in style it had produced; as he put it, the 'French style was more evolutionary' than the Americans. Moreover, the HR function from the centre was not actively pushing corporate policies on to its operations in other countries, and did not appear to be 'used to HR having a proactive role'. In two of the British firms there also appeared to be a decentralised approach to managing their acquired operations in other countries. In UKPower, two representatives of corporate HR described the way in which companies acquired in Germany and the USA were left as largely free standing business units, with HR involvement extending only to keeping an eye on the pension fund and some limited management development work. Similarly in BritBank, a British-owned financial services group, the acquisition of a French bank had not been followed by much change in HR policies, and there was only limited mobility of managers across the UK and France.

The French and British oil companies presented an opportunity to probe these issues in more depth. As described above, both firms undertook some major acquisitions in the late 1990s, significantly increasing their size and the scale of their international operations in particular. Yet they both remain strongly rooted in their original home bases. At EuroFuel, the French firm, we explored whether there was anything particularly French about the merger in comparison, say, to Anglo-

> '... the handling of HR decisions in different countries overwhelmingly reflected local influences, ...'

Saxon mergers. Respondents argued that there were four important differences:

- First, one of the major issues here centred on the sense of corporate identity and brand image, which is perhaps best illustrated by the decision to maintain the original company names within the new merged company for some time after the mergers. One senior management respondent commented on the ugliness of the new company's name, which was for some time an amalgamation of the different parties to the merger:

    What a horrible, horrible unimaginative name. The reason for that is there's a lot of possessiveness about the brand. In France they still maintain two brands and they're running two quite distinct networks, which again, if you were looking at any American, Anglo-Saxon-type acquisition, there's no way I can imagine Esso buying another company and then maintaining the brand name.

- Second, the British HR director referred to the French influence and what he called continental compromises in the merger process. One of the clearest examples was around the issue of balance in terms of the senior management team. In his words:

    It wasn't the kind of Anglo-Saxon deal where you wipe out the company that you acquired. They were determined in both cases to call them mergers ... so they were looking for balance all the time in terms of the management team. ... It was a continental compromise where we ended up on the face of it with [a mixture of people from each of the parties to the merger].

- Third, more speculatively, it would appear that the handling of HR decisions in different countries overwhelmingly reflected local influences, notwithstanding the intention of the centre to ensure balance in the selection of people for key positions. Thus this is another contrast with the more centralised approach of American companies.

- Fourth, and more substantially, senior corporate HR respondents argued that another way in which the merger differed from Anglo-Saxon mergers was in the extent of cost savings promised at the time of the merger. These were not as significant as is common in mergers involving British and American firms, owing to the political sensitivity of the issue of cost savings. Consequently, the overall headcount reduction was less stark than we found in the British and American companies that we studied, with involuntary redundancies kept to a minimum.

In the British oil company (BritOil) there was an evident requirement to realise cost savings. Senior management put a lot of emphasis on delivering cost savings and it was seen as imperative to deliver against these targets. Ongoing operational targets had been missed and this meant that integration savings needed to be recovered as quickly as possible. As one respondent put it in commenting on the pressure to realise cost savings, 'We needed some early wins, some measurable cost savings early in the process.' This context drove some tough decisions on redundancies and closures. Two of the recent acquisitions of North-American-based firms had led to a large number of job cuts. The acquisition of a specialist British firm also took place in this context, although the cost savings were never likely to be as great as it was motivated by a

> '... American firms tend to be more centralised and hands-on in the management of acquired units ...'

strategic move into a new market. This is clearly in marked contrast to the approach we saw in EuroFuel.

In conclusion, this chapter has thrown some light on the influence of the nationality of the parent firm in international M&As. One key finding was that American firms tend to be more centralised and hands-on in the management of acquired units, pushing corporate policies onto these units and looking to realise cost savings quickly. However, there was some variation between companies within the same country. The different organisational cultures at BritOil and another British firm that it acquired are one illustration of this, as is discussed in more detail later in the report.

Likewise, the picture among the seven American firms was a little more complex than this broad approach suggests. For example, FastFood, a company that has a reputation in the industry for a clear and distinctive 'corporate way' was surprisingly 'hands-off' in handling its acquisition in the UK, perhaps because the new unit was in a new line of business. In the two IT firms there was also relatively little direct influence from the corporate centre. In TeleCo this was mainly because the American ownership was only a minority stake, but in IT Services it applied even in wholly owned subsidiaries. One part of the explanation for this was that the parent firm was adopting a deliberately hands-off approach in the belief that managers in the acquired unit would work best if left to their own devices, but another part of the explanation appeared to be the Transfer of Undertakings Protection of Employment (TUPE) regulations that limited management's freedom to make changes to terms and conditions. It is to the effects of such characteristics of host countries to which we turn in the next chapter.

4 | Host country effects: comparing a merged company's HR practices in different countries

The sources of 'host country effects'

Having indicated the influence of the home country in the previous chapter, here we move to a consideration of so-called *host country effects*. In other words, we explore how the national context shapes the process of restructuring at national subsidiary or site level. There are a number of aspects of host systems that constrain the changes an acquiring firm is able to make to acquired units:

- legal obligations specifically relating to M&As such as TUPE in the UK

- requirements to negotiate the impact of mergers with bodies such as the Works Councils in Germany and to agree a Social Plan with this body

- the role of unions and collective bargaining systems in shaping the form of restructuring and changes in employment practices

- the more general notion of *national culture* in setting limits to what acquiring firms can do without losing the goodwill of staff, customers and the wider community.

In order to shed light on these host country effects we conducted interviews in a number of different countries: in BritOil comparisons were made between Britain and Spain; in EuroFuel interviews were conducted in Britain, France and Germany; and in GlobalDrug data were gathered from comparable plants in the USA, UK, Germany and Spain. The findings indicate a range of issues, such as the pace of integration on pay, the process of rationalisation of networks, and the introduction of new practices. The influence of the national environment is clearly discernible, conditioning what happens in the post-merger period, but as we will see there is often a certain amount of freedom within these constraints.

Institutional and cultural influences

The acquisition by BritOil of a specialist British firm has been played out with varying emphases in different countries, reflecting national institutional and cultural variations. In advance of the research we had expected that the stronger, more cohesive legal frameworks would present barriers to integration, causing it to be slower and less complete. However, the case revealed the relative lack of integration in the USA, reflecting the more permissive legal context in comparison to continental Europe. As one senior HR manager from the UK described it:

In terms of harmonisation I think it is only the USA that hasn't harmonised. The whole of Europe is harmonised … . The USA … is far removed from both of the former headquarters, and they were not in a hurry or not under as much pressure as we were here because there was no legal requirement to do it in the States, whereas in many countries in Europe it was a legal requirement that if you are the same legal entity you must have the same terms and conditions, so there was a different kind of push.

This is not to suggest that cultural, as opposed to legal, integration is necessarily easier in a highly legislated environment, and respondents from BritOil were keen to assert that the opposite can be the case. What they stressed as most important is that HR must have the capability to adapt the process to the diverse demands of varying local cultures, practices and laws.

> '... most important is that HR must have the capability to adapt the process to the diverse demands of varying local cultures, practices and laws.'

We can also see in this case the influence of pragmatic management decisions, and the way in which the difficulty of dealing with the implications of national differences often results in issues not being addressed and differences remaining. Some reasons for this are the lack of adequate due diligence, insufficient planning for integration and the absence of effective retention plans. For this point of view, *pragmatic* may be more a state of chaos than a deliberate strategy. In BritOil the same manager observed that

A couple of very senior HR people [from the acquired unit] left, and those posts were filled with people with very limited experience and virtually none at harmonisation, and it was just delay upon delay upon delay. And then we found out that the cost of converting [employees] to [BritOil] USA terms and conditions was extraordinarily high. There were issues with the pension fund being underfunded in the acquired unit, so the cost would have been astronomical, so that pushed it back even further.

We are not suggesting here that the lack of a natural successor to replace a senior HR manager was the major cause of the delay in the USA, but merely that having the wrong HR person can clearly slow down the process.

The distinct influence of particular national contexts in shaping post-merger restructuring is perhaps most clearly illustrated in the case of EuroFuel. In Germany, one of the parties to the merger was much larger than the others and consequently it served as the model for integration with many HR processes largely being imposed on the other parties, and the new HQ being located at its former HQ in Berlin. The German part of the company has had a very close relationship with the works council, setting up a Social Plan and engaging in a very close dialogue with what the HR manager described as *maximum transparency*. He described how the provision of information on corporate strategy to the Works Council helped to avoid subsequent complaints from employees who might have felt left behind in the process, as well as avoiding individual complaints to lawyers. In any case, the Works Councils in Germany are very strong and strict, and the HR manager considered their approval for post-merger changes to be a 'requirement under the "partnership" approach'. Moreover, the fact that the merger involved one company that was embedded in the east of the country had particular implications, given that German labour law is effectively divided into two parts. (One respondent commented how a Hamburg to Munich move would have been far more straightforward than Dusseldorf to Berlin.) A consequence of this consultative, partnership-based approach was that there were very few job cuts, some voluntary severance and a high post-merger retention rate.

The Works Councils and unions have also been very influential in France, affecting the timing and pace of the restructuring and integration. The firm was anxious to issue new contracts of employment across the firm, but faced strong resistance in the refineries that belonged to one of the parties to the merger. Workers and their unions were able to use their legal powers to refuse to sign up to the new contracts, meaning that a number of sets of terms and conditions continue to coexist. The extent and pace at which job cuts were made was also strongly shaped by the legislative environment. One senior manager commented on the difference between France and the UK in this respect:

Where you can make them [redundancies] is interesting ... The French, they are getting there

with their workforce. They are reducing but it's a much gentler process, much slower … . [The UK is] a pretty harsh environment when you compare it to some of the rest of Europe – much of the rest of Europe, I'd say. It's not very protective. On the other hand … in France you've got to hang around for ever and a day before you get your package.

The requirement to engage with the national institutional system of regulation also impacts upon the initial merger discussions and the timing of announcements – something that was particularly evident in the case of the EuroFuel merger as the dominant player was French. To quote the same senior UK manager:

There were a lot of union negotiations in France about [the merger]…. so for a couple of months we were kept hanging around in the UK being ready to do things, the staff knowing we were ready to do things, and all we could say was 'Sorry, we can't do any more'. We couldn't announce any organisation chart, which was just one of the things meaning Did you have a job or not? We couldn't do any of that until the unions in France had signed off.

Host country effects as barriers to integration

We outlined in the previous chapter how the GlobalDrug merger involved a significant degree of centralisation, reflecting in many respects the dominant influence of the model of the Anglo-American party to the merger (hereafter referred to as Anglo-American). A number of respondents described what central policies meant in HR terms, with the following issues being identified at the outset as those over which there would be a good deal of central influence:

◘ the spirit of the company
◘ pay for performance
◘ talent identification
◘ leadership development.

One respondent, when asked about the extent to which the merged company had international HR policies, and whether these resembled either party to the merger, replied, 'We have them, they're international and they're from Anglo-American,' and went on to say that the British firm had been much more a 'federation of independent business units that weren't governed by common policies'. One senior manager described the way in which the move towards a centralised model had created an impression of ever-more influential corporate HQ functions; many of the initiatives emanating from HQ 'are perceived as global company policy because the people behind them would love them to be global company policy, but … they're not, they're optional … This is where a lot of the fear, a lot of the confusion existed and to some extent still does.'

The shift towards a centralised model presented significant challenges to those sites that used to belong to the decentralised British-based firm. The merger had catapulted them into a position where suddenly they had a number of corporate-level HR policies to comply with, as well as dealing with the enhanced pressures to cut costs that stemmed from the promised cost savings at the time of the merger. Our case study incorporated four plants that belonged to the British firm, and looked at the ways in which they responded to these changed circumstances in general, and the role of the national institutional and cultural context in particular. The findings reveal some clear host country effects.

> 'National-level regulations and institutions can be rather more malleable than might appear at first sight.'

Perhaps the clearest of these was in relation to the issue of pay for performance. Following the merger, the influential corporate HR department indicated that there should be a link between pay and performance across the company. While there was an acknowledgement that this could vary by country, there was a demand that the site or division stretched the norms in their environment. As one person put it, 'If the norm in your country was that 10 per cent of pay is at risk, we would expect you to have 15 per cent. In other words we want to be at the top end of the pay for performance element.' In practice, this was difficult to implement in some countries. On the German site, for instance, the Works Council was able to use its legal powers to block any direct link between individual performance and pay, so that the policy takes the form of a bonus assessed on the performance of the site. This bonus had to be introduced in a way that did not threaten pre-existing base pay, again at the Works Council's insistence, and therefore, added to the costs of the site.

The malleability of national regulations and traditions

However, the case study also revealed the limitations of national-level constraints and the room for manoeuvre that MNCs enjoy, even in highly regulated countries. This was very well illustrated at the Spanish site. In Spain the national collective agreement for the chemical industry can be legally enforced across the sector, including pharmaceuticals factories. Thus, potentially, this agreement could have significantly constrained the possible courses of action at site level. However, the GlobalDrug site was located in an area that was traditionally non-union, and very few site employees were union members. Moreover, the national collective agreement set pay rates that were generally low; most unionised firms have supplementary site bargaining and non-unionised ones normally pay above this rate anyway. In fact, the Spanish plant faced fewer obligations to consult and negotiate with their workforce than did the British plant, despite the absence of national collective bargaining in the UK. National-level regulations and institutions can be rather more malleable than might appear at first sight.

In addition, the national-level factors were often less significant than those factors that are specific to the organisation. One of these is the structure of the company. While many international HR policies are global in their coverage, others apply only to the USA and UK, where slightly over half of the firm's employees are located. A consequence of this, given the strong American flavour to corporate HR activity was that when compared with the Spanish and German plants, the British site we examined had to deal with more policies coming from a higher level in the company.

Another organisational-level factor that strongly influences the impact of restructuring and changes in the post-merger period is the expertise held at each site and the performance of these sites. The cuts to employment levels and the closure of sites was strongly shaped by the centre's classification of plants according to their capabilities and whether they were set to play a key role in the newly merged network, for example in bringing a new product to the market or in producing for national markets with a demanding product regulator. Thus after the merger there followed a fraught, tense process of evaluation of all 100-plus sites, with key staff in the sites lobbying hard to protect their own patch. It was this political process rather than the national regulatory system of employment relations that seemed to be the key factor in shaping this aspect of the post-merger period.

In this chapter we have examined the role of national level factors in creating host country effects. These have included the need to establish a social plan and negotiate closely with Works Councils in Germany and the strength of French labour law in shaping the speed and nature with which terms and conditions can be integrated in merged companies. These effects are clearly considerable, and managing to strike a balance between working within the constraints they pose and yet simultaneously working towards integration and rationalisation is a key challenge for HR professionals in international M&As. However, we have also seen that national institutions and regulations are sometimes more malleable than they might appear to an outsider, giving merged firms some scope to minimise their influence. We have also flagged up the importance of organisational rather than solely national factors in shaping the nature of restructuring in international M&As. It is two of these – the nature of corporate structures and the processes of organisational politics – to which we turn in the next two chapters.

5 | Organisational structures and cultures: the impact of mixed heritage in mergers

Types of integration

In considering both *home* and *host* country influences, we have seen the impact of different national systems and cultures on merger processes. In this chapter we move from national to *organisational* structures and cultures, examining how the particular ways that companies have operated prior to merger affects the ease with which the transition towards a new corporate identity is made. In their different ways, all of our case-study organisations provide illustrative examples of the impact of *mixed heritage* in the newly merged organisation. A range of outcomes were apparent in terms of the way that merged firms evolved. One route was for different structures and cultures to continue to coexist in different parts of the merged organisation. In other words, there was relatively little integration between the two parts of the merged firm. An alternative route was for pressures for integration to be strong and for the firm to move towards the structure and culture of one of the organisations in a process of assimilation. A third possibility was for integration to occur with the merger presenting the opportunity for the firm to move towards a quite different structure and culture from those that characterised either of the firms prior to the merger.

The varying pressures towards integration

The strength of pressures to integrate varied across firms and sectors. This was strongly in evidence during the first phase of the research project. There was clearly variability in the extent to which the acquirer (or larger party in a merger) looked to exert influence over HR in the acquired operations, ranging from a hands-off approach to a more concerted attempt to apply common HR policies across the merged firm. This variability in part reflects the motivations for the M&A:

- Many mergers are motivated by a desire to move into new geographical markets or new lines of business. Where this is the case, the acquiring firm or larger party to the merger is unlikely to move quickly towards strong integration, partly because the incentives to do so are limited, but also because it may want to observe and learn from its acquisition. This is particularly the case in sectors that operate in quite different ways across borders, and this shows up strongly in the two utilities firms and, to an extent also, in the two financial sector firms.

- In a number of cases there was pressure for integration, if there was to be significant rationalisation and if duplication were to be avoided. Many M&As are justified on the basis of two broadly similar firms benefiting from the scale of joining forces, and from the opportunities for concentrating production in a smaller number of locations in order to achieve cost savings. In these cases, a degree of integration is required and common structures, and subsequently common practices, apply across the firms. This was very evident in the two pharmaceuticals firms and to a degree in the two oil firms.

In the remainder of this chapter we expand on these issues of mixed heritage in one of the oil firms and one of those in the pharmaceuticals sector, examining the complexities and tensions in the integration processes.

> 'The strength of pressures to integrate varied across firms and sectors.'

The dominance of the American heritage at GlobalDrug

The case of GlobalDrug throws up a particularly interesting instance of the impact of mixed heritage in merged firms, since it was billed very much as a 'merger of equals'. The merger was justified partly on the basis of the opportunity to realise cost savings from duplicate functions that could be streamlined but also on the increased scale that would allow the firm to build a large and powerful research and development (R&D) base. However, the scale of this part of the business presented some challenges for the company.

One concern was that the R&D division would be so large that it would become overly bureaucratic, and innovation would be stifled. In response to this concern, senior management introduced a structure that had not been part of either company prior to the merger, that involved six semi-autonomous units. These were organised around particular types of drug and were set up so as to allow managers within each unit to manage their workforces in ways that they saw fit, with pay and benefits packages varying according to the labour market pressures for each particular occupation and region. The plan was that these units would foster an entrepreneurial spirit that would emulate the fast-moving biotechnology companies and that those scientists involved in bringing a new drug to market would be rewarded handsomely for so doing. In practice, there have been some limitations to the amount of autonomy that the units have enjoyed, but their creation represents a form of integration based on an entirely new structure rather than on the structures that existed in either party to the merger.

In general, though, the HR organisation in GlobalDrug closely resembles that of the Anglo-American firm. A key part of this is the structure of the function; while the British firm was organised mainly around 'geographic silos' with HR structured on a country-by-country basis, Anglo-American's structure was formed around globally integrated businesses and functions. Between the merger being announced and it being completed, a decision was apparently taken by very senior managers that the new company would move towards the globally integrated model. One immediate implication of this concerned the filling of senior HR positions in the newly merged firm. Those individuals who had experience of operating internationally were clearly well placed to get the top jobs and indeed it is people from Anglo-American that dominate the HR function at senior levels in GlobalDrug.

Another set of implications that flowed from the adoption of a globally integrated model concerns the nature of HR policies. Apart from the use of IT systems in the HR function, most respondents struggled to think of HR policies that had come from the British party to the merger. In contrast, there are a number of areas where policies closely resemble those of Anglo-American. For instance, a particular area of HR policy that illustrates this is pay, Anglo-American operating with a higher proportion of pay at risk and lower base pay than its British counterpart (BritMediCo). The movement has been towards Anglo-American on this issue. One respondent described how this move stemmed from 'a fairly quick decision at board level'. Another noted how the new company puts more emphasis on rewarding good performance with financial bonuses, whereas previously in BritMediCo there was more of an emphasis on status. More generally, on pay and conditions, another respondent felt that

> '… it is people from Anglo-American that dominate the HR function at senior levels in GlobalDrug.'

Anglo-American had been working much more effectively … as a global organisation, had a global approach to HR issues and therefore things like grading structures, common terms and conditions and common philosophies lower down the organisation.

It had, for example, a global grading scheme for middle managers and above, which would directly impact upon benefits received, particularly share options.

There were other more general changes to management style that appeared to reflect the Anglo-American influence. One respondent described how BritMediCo had a greater tendency to negotiate changes and implement them gradually, whilst Anglo-American's approach was to implement changes more quickly. There also appeared to be much more emphasis on financial performance, particularly quarterly results. As one person put it:

I think the company is much more hard-nosed than BritMediCo was. I think that BritMediCo had the overall philosophy that if you do the right things, financial results will be following. I think the GlobalDrug view is 'Do the things that will drive the financial results and hopefully most of them will be right', which is more than a subtle change … . [And] there is no doubt from my observation that Anglo-American were more financially driven than BritMediCo. They reported quarterly whereas BritMediCo reported half-yearly. Anglo-American were more Americanised. … What we are doing now is seeing the more Americanised, financially-driven way of running a corporation than we saw in BritMediCo which was done in more of the British way.

The rationale for this shift to a globally integrated model concerned the growing need to co-ordinate operations across borders in a sector where products closely resemble one another and where the main competitors also employ globally integrated structures. Some former BritMediCo managers and employees approved of the shift, arguing that some of the sites had operated like fortresses, unwilling to engage in transferring expertise with the rest of the company, concentrating on running their own 'domains and fiefdoms'. In contrast, Anglo-American was seen as more integrated, bonded at the seams and with more shared learning. However, one problem was that the shift towards the Anglo-American model was perceived by some as being at odds with a deal that was portrayed as a merger of equals. Many respondents were quite clear that 'It was not a merger, it was a takeover by Anglo-American', and that while early on it was communicated as a merger of equals it soon became clear that it was the Anglo-American 'legacy folks' who were 'driving the bus'. Some former BritMediCo employees expressed this more strongly, commenting that 'You can call it a merger of equals if you like, but basically we're sold out.'

Culture clash and compromise at BritOil

Just as the GlobalDrug merger brought together two different types of organisation, so too did the acquisition of the specialist British firm (SpecialityCo) by BritOil. There were a number of marked differences between the two firms:

- Whereas BritOil had a substantial presence in a number of countries but was scarcely present in a number of others, SpecialityCo had built up a small presence in a large number of countries.

> '... some of the sites had operated like fortresses, unwilling to engage in transferring expertise with the rest of the company ...'

- The SpecialityCo model was one of a fairly loose federation with local managers having a good deal of autonomy over organisational practices while BritOil had a stronger degree of international integration.

- One aspect of the culture in SpecialityCo was of formal hierarchy shaping many aspects of HR practice, particularly pay and benefits, while BritOil was more egalitarian.

- In terms of international HR, policies across SpecialityCo owed a lot to what country managers had managed to negotiate with their bosses, whereas in BritOil there is more emphasis on formal, written policies.

Many of the merger integration issues and challenges at BritOil have arisen as a direct consequence of these different pre-existing corporate structures and associated corporate philosophies. However, unlike in GlobalDrug where the approach has been a fairly rapid convergence on the structures, policies and culture of one of the parties to the merger, BritOil's approach to these structural differences has been much more gradual.

One illustration of this is in the USA. While the lubricants business in the States is primarily ex-SpecialityCo, these operations are now considered 'part of the club now ... [and there is] a set of ways we expect people to do things when they're part of the club'. One way in which BritOil moved towards greater uniformity is through the implementation of a standardised IT system, by which one model now operates throughout the world and every manager has the same piece of technology, and uses standard procurement and standard software, which is fully interchangeable. Here again, the price of integration and uniformity was an increase in costs. To a certain extent there was a resistance to this integration in the USA: 'They found it very difficult in America, saying that's going to cost us too much. Why can't we go to our local IT store where we can buy a PC for this amount of money?' But the trend is clear:

There's been a lot of physical integration, which didn't take place in the immediate month or two before we integrated, and after it's still going on, it's making us very much mainstream BritOil, rather than this outpost called SpecialityCo.

In HR one immediate source of concern was over the handling of redundancies. Faced with some suspicion from SpecialityCo staff of the approach BritOil might take, BritOil management had to convince them that such issues would be dealt with fairly. Even once trust is established, an ongoing issue has been the impact of the SpecialityCo tradition of decentralisation and hierarchy, with powerful chief executives having a good deal of local autonomy, whilst BritOil has traditionally been more co-ordinated and less hierarchical. One senior manager summed this up as follows:

I think it depends on the underlying philosophy of the corporations ... how you are towards people and situations. I would describe BritOil as in principle about equality and fairness, not that I'm saying SpecialityCo is about inequality ... [but in] SpecialityCo you differentiate according to hierarchy, and when you were treating a senior person it was different from how you are treating somebody more junior in the organisation ... and the rewards of these employees are actually quite different.

The manager responsible for integration in the Asia-Pacific region indicated a number of

> '...an ongoing issue has been the impact of the SpecialityCo tradition of decentralisation and hierarchy ...'

instances. One of these concerned open-plan offices. While these were seen as a threat by some senior ex-SpecialityCo staff, apparently because they eroded traditional hierarchical differences, BritOil saw them as an important symbolic move towards creating a more federal culture, relying more on peer groups and networks. Thus the acquirer has insisted on this change. This issue touches particular nerves in countries where status and hierarchy are still very important to people. Another instance was around job titles. A *sales manager* in BritOil was considered to be equivalent to a SpecialityCo *sales director*, but when there was a move to change the latter group's job titles to match those at BritOil, a number of SpecialityCo employees locally felt they were being demoted. They were eventually allowed to keep their job titles, and so differences remain on this issue.

This mix of significant change and pragmatic acceptance of inherited practices also shows through in relation to pay. The two approaches to pay had previously been significantly different: in BritOil, pay and benefits were more 'egalitarian', as one manager described it, and there was an influential variable pay programme, whereas SpecialityCo was more hierarchical with an individual's pay package resting partly on their formal status and partly on what they personally were able to negotiate. The evidence of pragmatism was that the process of co-ordinating pay packages within the newly merged company worked on the principle that no ex-SpecialityCo employee would be worse off for the first two years in terms of their total package. Particular elements were to change, however, often in ways that signified BritOil's moves to bring about a significant change in the culture. For example, in Japan the integration manager said that SpecialityCo managers 'used to get all kinds of bonuses', and BritOil moved to link these much more directly to performance pay. Similarly, in Malaysia many senior SpecialityCo people were unhappy that they had developed a scheme for the top 25 'high potentials', which was not a definition that BritOil shared, and this group lost some of their benefits.

The two companies had differing approaches to recruitment and development, reflected in these diverging conceptions of high potential employees. One of the senior HR managers involved in the integration process observed that

half or more of the people identified as high potential in SpecialityCo were external mature hires from outside of the oil industry. BritOil historically grows its own wood, so if you look at a BritOil high potential list, it is going to be populated by people who started their career in BritOil or people who were acquired over the years. That was a very big cultural difference, I think … So in a strange way it slowed down integration.

This gradual assimilation has meant that there is a feeling of 'business as usual' for many ex-SpecialityCo employees; there was an impression that many of this group thinks that life hasn't changed too much.

In conclusion, these two detailed case studies throw up quite different approaches to integration. Whereas in GlobalDrug there was a clear and rapid move towards the structure, culture and policies of one of the parties to the merger, in BritOil-SpecialityCo the process was much more gradual. What was evident in both cases, however, and in different ways in all of the case studies that we conducted, were the sensitivities involved in international M&As. The periods just before, and particularly just after, a merger or acquisition are

> **'What was evident in both cases, however, and in different ways in all of the case studies ... were the sensitivities involved in international M&As.'**

times when a variety of groups seek to defend or advance their own causes in a bid to make sure that the form that integration takes does not challenge their interests. Thus, these periods are highly political, and this is the subject of Chapter 6.

6 | The process and politics of mergers: timing, resistance and compromise

The political dimension to international M&As

The consideration of mixed heritage in the case-study organisations has raised a number of issues to do with the political dimension of M&As. While there is considerable diversity across the case studies in the way in which HR issues have been handled, in all of the companies this political dimension is visible in the merger process. The periods immediately before and after the merger are when a lot is up for grabs – issues such as the filling of key positions and the structure of the new company or division that have lasting impacts on individuals and groups. Hence, this time is inevitably fraught with tensions, and political battles occur as individuals and groups seek to advance their interests. This is not to say that systematic assessments and plans do not feature. Rather, this approach is complemented by various parties to the merger having different priorities and using whatever resources they possess to achieve their goals. The international dimension to M&As is highly significant in this respect because knowledge of, and familiarity with, the peculiarities of national systems can be used as a source of influence by those who wish to shape the merger process. The politics of the post-merger period in international M&As show up in various ways, and this chapter explores a number of aspects of this.

The persistence of pre-existing corporate identities

The two oil companies provided instances of staff continuing to identify with their former employer and colleagues. Some of these may appear trivial, but in fact reflect deep tensions. For example, one source of potential or actual conflict in M&As is between sets of employees who were previously in competition with one another. For many employees this does not arise since they do not come into contact with those with whom they were previously in competition. Production workers in the two pharmaceuticals firms are in this category. However, in customer-facing roles this is more of an issue. The prime illustration of the legacy of previously competitive relationship is from the French oil firm. The two French parties to the merger had been bitter competitors for several decades and here integrating HQ staff was a fraught process. The company owns two towers in the business district of Paris, one from each of the two firms, and moving staff between the towers became a symbolic barrier across which some were reluctant to jump. In the UK, employees from the different parties to the merger continue to socialise – mainly with their former colleagues. Many petrol station managers were opposed to a rebranding which resulted in the loss of their original firm's name (hence the compromise that produced the mouthful of a name) and the location of the British HQ became a touchstone aspect of the mergers. This latter issue was subject to a consultation exercise in the hope that the decision would be seen to be fair, although some within the firm saw this exercise as having little real influence on the outcome. As one respondent put it, 'The MD and his wife had already decided [where they wanted to live].'

In the British oil company there was also evidence of those in the acquired company resisting incorporation into the new company. Some of this centred on the brand name. One respondent from the acquired organisation described the way in which many of his colleagues continued to use

> 'While ... focus on balance was important at the very top of the organisation, it appeared to have less influence within functions such as HR ...'

the former brand name on their business cards and email addresses, and how his boss had been active in preserving the brand name for fear that its disappearance would adversely affect morale. As he put it:

I was prohibited by my boss from giving a BritOil business card to any SpecialityCo heritage person to use in any official capacity in the business because of the diluted focus on the brand, etc, etc. So there was a tremendously strong attempt by a lot of the SpecialityCo heritage leadership to keep BritOil out because they said it would be demotivating.

Much of this reflects the significant business model and brand philosophy differences between the two merging organisations. The acquisition was very much an acquisition of brand and marketing capability. Whilst the SpecialityCo heritage leaders had translated that capability deeply into the organisation, the BritOil heritage leaders tended not to grasp the significance of this. As some of the respondents argue elsewhere, a deeper and broader due diligence process could have uncovered the criticality of this difference.

Selection of people for senior positions

In those cases where one company did not dwarf the other, positions on the management board of the newly merged company were allocated partly on the basis of an even distribution between the parties to the merger. In the French oil company, which had undergone two large mergers in a year or so, one manager described the way that 'the firm was looking for balance all the time in terms of the management team'. The UK operations of each company in the first of the two mergers that occurred three years previously were roughly the same size, and so following the merger there were four people from each of the parties to the merger on the new management board. Then, when the second merger occurred, the management board was changed again so as to incorporate two people from the third party to the new firm. The qualities of individuals were obviously factors in selection, but the process was also strongly influenced by the desire to have *balance* in order to keep groups in both parts of the company happy.

The creation of the management board following a merger of two roughly equal-sized firms also appeared to be a political process in GlobalDrug. As we have already seen, the merger was billed as a merger of equals, and this meant that positions on the senior management board were allocated proportionately between the two firms, rather than solely on merit. One important implication was to do with the quality of people appointed. One respondent at GlobalDrug argued that filling positions in this way could lead to a 'complete dingbat' being appointed (though he was anxious to stress that this had not been the case in the current merger). There was also a strong emphasis on the appointment of country MDs being seen as open and not favouring one or other party. While this focus on balance was important at the very top of the organisation, it appeared to have less influence within functions such as HR; as described in Chapter 5, in GlobalDrug people from one of the parties to the merger dominate senior HR positions.

BritOil similarly sought to maintain a sense of balance in staffing decisions, and by their own admission, 'sometimes ended up with crude-looking processes'. That said, each party to a merger will tend to have its own tradition of selection, and a unique process can be more

> '... the firm selling the operations can continue to have an influence over how HR issues are handled, even some time after the transfer ...'

acceptable to more people. Moreover, as one senior HR manager commented,

The HR professional during this phase needs the capability to create processes that are fair, simple, transparent, balanced, etc, giving less attention to speed, efficiency, etc. An ugly-looking process can pay big dividends if it meets both the needs of the Co. for the best talent, and the mood of the people in the selection pool(s).

In addition, this case study provides an interesting case of how deals done at the time of the merger evolve over time. Following the acquisition, the design of the leadership teams for each of the businesses was structured partly around the issue of balance. As one respondent put it, 'The importance of getting good balance in the teams – one man from SpecialityCo, one man from BritOil – something like balance was important.' Co-HR directors for the whole division were appointed, one from each side, to oversee the integration process more generally. For some months two people co-ordinated closely to conduct HR during this period. Eventually, however, the person from the acquired organisation stood aside, acknowledging that his co-HR director had stronger links with those outside the division in the rest of the company, and that therefore he was the natural person to assume sole charge of the function.

The role of external stakeholders

A further illustration of the political nature of the post-merger period relates to the role of external firms and bodies that have a degree of influence over the merger process. The case of IT Services is a good example of how the firm selling the operations can continue to have an influence over how HR issues are handled, even some time after the transfer has taken place. This firm, American in origin, has grown significantly in recent years through gaining contracts from the outsourcing of IT operations by other companies, including many from the public sector. In gaining so many of these outsourcing contracts it inherited lots of different sets of terms and conditions, and the firm's ability to harmonise these was significantly constrained not only by the TUPE regulations but also by a need to keep the selling firm happy. One might expect the selling firm not to be concerned about this, but in the case of the public sector particularly, contracting out to professional staff has been highly contentious. To stand any chance of winning further contracts, IT Services needed to reassure the government that the transfers would be handled smoothly, avoiding protests from staff and unions that they had been adversely affected. Thus the company had to tread carefully in managing the restructuring in order to keep the staff and unions, and therefore also the government, 'on board'. Consequently, the restructuring was not governed solely by a rational assessment of where changes should ideally come, and management has been very pragmatic in accepting practices that they inherited.

Governments can also influence the merger process through their regulatory agencies. An illustration of this is at GlobalDrug. A crucial aspect of the pharmaceutical industry is the need to get regulatory approval to sell in a national market. Many regulatory bodies are influenced by governments into preferring production to take place in their own country rather than relying on imports. This means that many pharmaceutical firms have considerable excess capacity, with plants in many countries operating well below their full potential. The merger was justified in part on the basis of significant cost savings from

> '... the outcome of this global-local question is not entirely the result of a rational, one-off assessment ... at the corporate HQ, but also is the product of ... political process of negotiation and compromise'

rationalisation of the manufacturing network, but in embarking on this process the firm has to keep the regulators on board, and this represented a constraint on the closure programme. Thus the political issue here is between the government and the firm rather than within the firm.

The global-local tension

In earlier chapters we have seen the way in which there is great variation in the extent to which international M&As lead to globally integrated firms or ones that exhibit a lot of national variation. One aspect of this that we only hinted at above is that the outcome of this global-local question is not entirely the result of a rational, one-off assessment by those at the corporate HQ, but also is the product of an ongoing political process of negotiation and compromise. At SnackCo, for instance, it was evident during the first few months following the merger that the parent company in America wanted to introduce a range of policies across their operations. However, over time it became clear that considerable flexibility was introduced into this global approach. For instance, on pay, the intention was to have standardised individual incentive plans. However, in many European countries those responsible for HR argued that they needed the approval from Works Councils and needed to negotiate any changes over time. The reaction from corporate and European HQ was a pragmatic one, accepting that many pre-existing practices should be left in place, but that all the managers in the acquired operations should move onto the new incentive programme.

The case of GlobalDrug also shows up the political dimension to the post-merger process of strengthening global HR policies and applying these to the previously largely decentralised British party to the merger. Our investigations of the four plants in different countries revealed that there was a degree of variation at this level as site HR (and other) managers used their familiarity with their particular circumstances to interpret policies in varied ways. In addition, on occasions, site HR managers would argue with the centre over the nature of a policy that caused them problems. One illustration of this was the policy on the use of *contingent* staff. Following a legal ruling in the USA, the British and American operations were not allowed to employ temporary staff continuously for more than 18 months. This caused some problems for one of the British sites that was experiencing a particularly busy time as a result of a number of product transfers. After protests from the site management team a temporary exception from this policy was allowed.

The nature of cost savings and restructuring

Many M&As are justified on the basis of cost savings, which will be realised through rationalisation. This is particularly the case at GlobalDrug where there had been over-capacity in both firms prior to the merger and both had a rationalisation programme in place. As noted above, one constraint on the closure programme in both firms was that it could be difficult to serve a national market without a manufacturing presence in that country, meaning that a site that was below capacity might be kept open anyway. The overlap in the merged firm made it much easier to close plants since the combined firm now had more than one in many countries, and the firm set a target of reducing the number of production sites by one-third within three years.

However, there were a number of complications in closing sites and transferring work across

> '... there were also indications of tensions between sites over formal product transfers.'

them. One of these is the requirement in the pharmaceuticals sector to obtain separate regulatory approval for the transfer of production to a new site for every single transfer. Approvals usually take months and can take as long as two years; given that the rationalisation programme involved around 30,000 product transfers over three years, this became a massive task. Further complications were added by the unpredictability of demand; one site that had been earmarked for closure suddenly became extremely busy as a competitor experienced technical problems with a rival product, with the result that the site received a stay of execution. Moreover, large manufacturing sites in most countries are heavily unionised and GlobalDrug's sites are no exception, meaning that there have been many lengthy processes of negotiation and consultation over proposed closures.

The restructuring was based around a system of 'site contracts' – every site was categorised into one of three types: 'new product introduction', which was the development of new products; 'mature products', which is high-volume, big selling products; and 'tail product' sites, which produced drugs that were in the decline phase or were being discontinued. In many cases it was straightforward which category a plant would go into, but it was not always the case. One of the North American sites had products in different categories and was described as 'in the tail-end of the middle category', and if they were not careful they would 'fall into the final category'. One respondent described another plant that supplies other pharmaceutical companies: 'Maybe there is a fourth category. It does not fit into any of the three categories.' This shows how the allocation was not a clear-cut rational judgement, but one that was open to argument, and plants could try and protect their position.

In addition, the complications of transferring products meant that the process of closing sites was slow, and in this context sites could try to position themselves as favourably as possible. Within regions of the company, pre-existing trading relationships appeared to have led to sites forming alliances with one another as they helped each other out by passing work between themselves, helping those that looked vulnerable to stay open. This did not really assist in the programme to close as many plants as possible, but was considered fair and legitimate by those engaging in the alliances. In contrast, there were also indications of tensions between sites over formal product transfers. One respondent described his site as a good 'group player', but complained that other sites failing to manage the transfer process competently had messed it around.

In this context, it is not surprising that there was a lot of lobbying from sites for the outcome of the review, and site contract decisions in particular. One respondent described the process in which sites were asked to do a 'site impact assessment'. She argued that the sites that were keen to get 'new product introduction status' had tried to do a lot of 'lobbying and influencing', though she went on to say that 'what impact or effect that will have is very hard to see'. Another respondent agreed that the HQ allowed relatively little influence from sites themselves in this process, though he argued that sites sometimes submitted 'skewed' data in order to get products transferred to them:

Subsequently you find that the site that said they could do it for nothing are asking for millions of pounds of capital expenditure, staff numbers are increasing, there is a whole additional amount of resource either because they had underestimated what it takes to do the additional production or maybe they just wanted to save their own skin.

He stressed the importance of sites being 'politically aware' and that each needs to 'fight its corner and some people do it better than others'. Thus while the restructuring process has been governed in a strategic way by the corporate HQ with clear criteria set out at the beginning, the process is still partly a political one.

In this chapter we have seen that the periods immediately before and after a merger or acquisition are characterised by a good deal of negotiation and compromise. With a lot of key issues to be sorted in a short space of time and an absence of established procedures and criteria for dealing with these issues, it is inevitable that there will be a number of informal deals and some horse-trading. This is especially the case in international M&As where the greater complexity in the environment gives individuals and groups grounds for putting forward a special case. This political aspect to the process shapes the way that particular HR issues are handled, and the role of the HR function more generally is influenced by the politics of international M&As. It is these two issues that we consider in turn in the next chapter.

7 | The HR role in mergers: key policy areas and the lessons learned

A range of policy issues

There is much evidence pointing to the importance of a wide range of HR policy areas that warrant consideration during a merger. The loss of staff is common and so retention is a key issue. The mobility of employees across the merged firm and the training required for this are also crucial areas. Pension, holiday and car entitlements are all potentially tricky issues with much uncertainty for employees. We have chosen in this chapter to highlight a few key areas that have come out most strongly from this particular research project. We focus on three areas:

- pay and benefits
- management selection and development
- harmonisation and integration.

We conclude the chapter with a brief summary of what respondents themselves felt were the key lessons for HR from their own experiences, particularly those issues that they would highlight for HR people going through the same process. Here we cover three issues:

- employee communication
- the pace of change
- the influence of the HR function.

Each of the issues addressed in this chapter is illustrated with a small number of quotes from respondents from across the case-study companies. Whilst we have stressed throughout this report that each case is different and that any merger process needs to be understood within a particular organisational context, there are nevertheless some issues that appear to have a more general applicability, as reflected by the unattributed nature of the quotes here.

Pay and benefits

This is an issue where there is an obvious tension when two companies merge. On the one hand the pre-existing differences in pay and benefits are immediately obvious to everyone involved in the merger process. In the light of this, a degree of harmonisation is required if people from each of the two firms are to work together. On the other hand, most aspects of pay and benefits are protected by TUPE, making harmonising *downwards* towards the more poorly paid group difficult whilst harmonising *upwards* towards the better paid group will be expensive. The result is often a series of compromises and a patchwork quilt of different sets of terms and conditions continuing for some time after the merger or acquisition. In general, this is exactly what our data reveal; most of the companies studied have adopted a highly pragmatic approach to this issue, though there was one notable exception.

This is the case even where the parent firm has a highly distinctive management style in its home country, as in the case of IT Services. Having grown almost entirely through acquisitions, the firm has 23 different sets of terms and conditions for its 18,000 workers in the UK. The indications were that while these would not be what management would have chosen (and the company certainly would not have chosen to negotiate with trade unions), it has accepted that things should stay pretty much as they are in order not to rock the boat and also in order to comply with TUPE. In firms that involve a number of groups of employees being transferred under a range of separate outsourcing deals, this is likely to be a common picture.

> '... integration has occurred more quickly and fully in the UK than in France.'

The EuroFuel case again demonstrates pragmatic responses in the way in which pay and benefits packages continue to differ across the merged firm. In this case, the differences in pay between the two merging firms are quite evident and moves towards integration have been slow. There was an evident tension in how quickly the firm could integrate its operations: given the strength of the unions in refining in France, employees would only accept the new terms and conditions if they were better off, and so getting everyone to agree would have been too expensive. Consequently, differences will continue to exist for the foreseeable future. What is interesting here is that integration has occurred more quickly and fully in the UK than in France.

And again at BritOil, different principles underlay the approaches of the merging companies towards pay. An attempt at integration was made, but this could not happen immediately and pre-existing arrangements continued for some time. The approach of one of the merging firms had very much been that reward is driven by performance of the asset, so that business performance is reflected in individual performance. In the other firm, by contrast, sales and customer-based targets drove rewards, so if targets were met as an individual, then rewards would follow. For two years following the merger there continued to be different packages, such that two people might have been working on exactly the same job at exactly the same level, with one receiving perhaps a 10 per cent variable pay payment and the other getting nothing. Subsequently there has been a gradual shift towards greater uniformity, with the policy of the dominant party to the merger taking precedence.

The GlobalDrug case, however, reveals a slightly less pragmatic approach to existing differences. While average pay was not massively different between the two merging companies, the way it was calculated was very different – high base pay and low bonuses in one firm, and low base pay and high bonuses in the other. The integration of pay was seen as an important way in which the new culture of the firm was to be created and diffused – linked to the Performance and Development Programme covering 11,000 of the most senior staff.

These efforts at integration mean that the pay scheme is now similar across the American operations. However, it very much reflects the dominance of the pre-existing approach of one of the parties to the merger. This meant that for professional and managerial people from the other firm there were a number of losers (in particular, the share option scheme did not cover as many people), but for shop-floor workers there was a less obvious impact. For those that have lost out on share options, though, there is a lot of dissatisfaction. Before the merger the US sites at GlobalDrug felt largely unaffected by global policies, with a strong country focus across R&D, manufacturing and commercial. After the merger there was much greater consistency, specifically between the USA and UK, and this meant that the previously autonomous American site now became subject to much greater HQ influence. For instance, in relation to compensation, many people lost cars and stock options as these have been confined to particular grades.

> 'The need to select and develop managers for senior positions is a crucial issue during M&As ...'

Management selection and development

The need to select and develop managers for senior positions is a crucial issue during M&As, which has been faced by all of the companies studied here.

As with the issue of pay, again there are pre-existing differences in emphasis that need to be worked through. At BritOil, for example, there were major differences in terms of training and development. One party to the merger was very focused on developing technical excellence, whilst the other focused much more on general management, general careers and career planning. The latter would develop long-term careers, bring people in at graduate level and develop them, whereas the former traditionally would recruit far more mature mid-career managers, buying in technical excellence from other organisations. At BritOil, a lot of emphasis was placed on getting *leadership teams* in place early on, and subsequently moving down through the organisational hierarchy to staff every level. Again it was considered crucial to ensure a good balance in the initial leadership teams, a process over which HR had considerable input and influence.

One aspect of management development that surfaced in all of the mergers studied was the need to quickly select people for senior posts. In GlobalDrug this involved the use of *cross interviews* and external consultants: senior managers reported that around 80 per cent of the appointment decisions were clear-cut, but 20 per cent involved some disagreement. Particular difficulties arose in appointing country managers, as someone from one of the heritage companies and not the other would fill these positions. A monitoring process was used to ensure that one company did not dominate in terms of senior appointments. The senior HR manager thus saw himself as 'the keeper of fairness', with the aim of arriving at a balance between the two companies in appointments to senior positions.

Some difficulties emerged in the selection of high-calibre people to run projects. For example, in the Asia Pacific region, in one of the heritage companies running a project would be seen in a positive light, whilst in the other the perception was often that it signalled a sidelining and possibly the end of a career. Consequently it was difficult to recruit high-calibre people from the latter company into joint project teams. That said, the senior HR manager in this region felt that progress had been greater than in Europe; the European part of the business struggled for some time to recruit a senior person with sufficient internal credibility to oversee the establishment of the leadership teams.

You need to find one or two people who have the talent and the passion, and hopefully some experience, to be internal change agents, and position them at a high level to be those internal architects ... [with an] appreciation of how important these soft factors are.

[The] lack of a credible lead person can hamper progress enormously.

There were timelines set and leadership teams defined .... Within 30 days after that you will have completely staffed the organisation, every appointment will have been made, every individual will know their outcome .... Because so much of the focus is put on that, some of the other things get put on the back burner.

> 'A ... key HR issue that is crucial to ensuring a smooth transition ... organisation is the handling of redundancies.'

Harmonisation and integration

Efforts at achieving balance in senior management teams and project teams highlight the more general issue of organisational integration – something which is especially challenging where the two parties to the merger have different established management cultures.

Respondents across the case-study companies agreed that whilst the search for balance is important, the reality is that one heritage company will tend to dominate and that resentment and resistance to change are to be expected. The challenge is to be able to move steadily towards a new culture through the development of key players who are committed to the new organisation's goals, and to utilise existing organisational differences as a mechanism for change.

There is a key role for HR here in terms of making an assessment or audit of cultural differences prior to merger. At BritOil the lack of this was felt to have hampered the smooth progress of integration. One senior manager reported that he was not aware of any 'bi–cultural diagnostics' or 'cultural due diligence' prior to the merger, the absence of which made the first year of the integration process far harder than it need have been.

The integration process throws up a range of difficult issues that are not easily resolved. Paramount here are changes to terms and conditions. At EuroFuel, for example, getting agreement to unifying terms and conditions has been a real struggle across the company, and particularly in France. This involved the merging of three sets of terms and conditions. Interestingly, the most emotive issue in the UK was around company car provision. The car scheme was effectively abandoned, which resulted in staff from one of the heritage companies losing out quite badly as they had been used to a generous car scheme. A further key HR issue that is crucial to ensuring a smooth transition towards the merged organisation is the handling of redundancies. A number of respondents spoke of the need to ensure that severance packages are developed and administered 'quickly and humanely', and also that steps are taken to recognise and deal with what one manager called 'survivor guilt'.

Our data allow us to comment also on the process by which integration typically occurs. Once again pragmatism appears to be the watchword. At BritOil, for example, each area of HR policy was examined and a decision taken on which aspects from each heritage company to keep and which to jettison. Two lists were made and arrows drawn by each area to indicate the extent to which the new policy would veer towards either of the two existing policies. Respondents argued that whilst there had been 'give and take in the actual outcomes, a compromise', nevertheless the 'default position' tends to be that of the dominant party to the merger.

The BritOil case also highlights the challenge, which all of the case-study companies faced, of harmonising terms and conditions across different countries. This was conducted on a country-by-country basis because, as a senior HR manager put it, 'in Europe especially the law varied greatly, and there was no way to do it in a pan-European way.' A network of managers was established to deal with this process, each country having its own integration team and an HR focal point.

> 'It is self-evident that communicating with employees during a merger is important ...'

It is about understanding subtle differences between the two firms and using this friction to really drive big change and really think fundamentally about how to reinvent the business.

People assume that just because it was a 'merger of equals' that things are equal, and I know personally I don't feel that way, and I think a lot of people did not think that way, much as we tried to articulate that view.

I don't think it has to be a deal-breaker, but it would certainly be helpful before you go in to Day 1 communication to have a clear understanding of the history and cultural background of the other organisation.

DON'T try to change everyone or everything. DO seek out and develop a core group of committed champions and support them as missionaries for change ... Operate on the principle of 'critical mass' – 20% committed can align 80% who are not (yet).

Employee communication

It is self-evident that communicating with employees during a merger is important, and indeed those involved in handling this issue stressed the importance of regular and meaningful communication throughout the pre- and post-merger periods. More substantively, there were three particular issues that were identified as being important factors bearing on the extent and form of communication.

One of these concerned the influence of European legislation on consultation. In GlobalDrug the process of consultation adopted in the case of plant closures and redundancies was described as a 'European model'. That is, the UK employees and their unions were afforded the same rights to consultation as their counterparts in more regulated environments such as Germany and France. This meant that the consultation periods were longer and involved more opportunities for unions to voice concerns, raise objections and make suggestions. As one senior HR manager described this: 'I might sound very high-minded, but actually it was a very pragmatic decision that we made, bearing in mind the number of shop stewards we deal with in the UK who are members of the European Works Council.'

National regulations concerning the nature of processes of consultation and negotiation were also in evidence in EuroFuel, but in this case they presented a number of challenges for UK-based managers. One instance of this was in the immediate post-merger period and concerned the announcement of the new structure of the company, an issue that had obvious implications for the number and type of managerial positions that would exist in the new company. While decisions at UK level were taken quite quickly, these had to be approved by the parent company and this would only happen when the French part of the company had agreed the organisational structure of the entire company with the unions in France. This took several months, leaving the rest of the company in limbo. The UK HR director described this as a 'frustrating time' and stressed the importance of both explaining the delay to British employees and ensuring that information did not leak out.

BritOil also faced similar challenges in wanting to communicate information to their employees in different countries at the same time, but having also to respect the national-level institutional

> 'There is always a balance to be struck between the need to move swiftly and the need to keep ... stakeholders ... on board'

requirements in place across their operations. This had implications for the pace at which changes were implemented, a subject we tackle in the next subsection.

We immediately started to communicate ... the ethical position that [the company] takes ... We immediately went to work ... to translate that document into the languages that we needed to, and get it out to everybody ... to use it as a way of drawing people together.

We must communicate with employees even if there is nothing to say.

The pace of change

One of the interesting issues we were able to explore was management views on the pace of change required during a merger. There is always a balance to be struck between the need to move swiftly and the need to keep various stakeholders (including employees) on board and to follow 'due process'.

On the latter point, the role of trade unions is pertinent. In some cases unions may need to be kept on board and have sufficient power to influence restructuring. For example, the slow pace of change at EuroFuel in France was put down to the strength of the French unions and regulations. This had knock-on effects in the UK, where many considered it to be unfair that they had been subject to a number of changes in a much shorter space of time, resulting in tensions between different national groups within the merged firm.

In BritOil there was a feeling among many senior managers that the early stages of the merger process had been too process-driven and over-planned, and that greater emphasis should have been placed on moving quickly as opposed to strictly following the detail of procedures. The filling of senior positions is an illustrative point. HR were involved in developing the criteria for selection, defining the pool, developing the redundancy terms and publicising the principles up front. As described earlier in the report, an advocacy approach was used for senior posts, involving a suggestion-and-challenge process and the use of career-direction statements for around 400 so-called *tier-3 managers*. In the event, however, hardly any of these statements were looked at and those involved reverted to far greater informality in order to move ahead at greater speed.

The BritOil case is also interesting as the company had been engaged in successive mergers over recent years. A number of managers spoke of the learning process involved, with the first big merger in 1998 feeling like 'walking through a blizzard', with 'a lot of us just making it up as we were going along'. Lessons were learned for the second merger and a greater degree of initial mapping out allowed for a smoother and quicker pace of change.

Speed is very important. The faster you can do it, the better it is for everybody. The process of culture could have been developed right from the start, and to try to get people to exhibit certain behaviours from the start.

Once you have understood what changes you need to make, make them as fast as possible ... Better to run helter-pelter and discover that you need to slightly adjust your course ... than let a gap develop between the organisation that acquired you and yourselves that you can't breach.

> 'A key factor ... was the integration of HR with top management and the business divisions ...'

I learned that it can actually work and intelligent people can pick it up as it goes along, so you don't need an exact plan up front.

The influence of the HR function

This research project has demonstrated the great contrasts between companies in terms of how systematic they are in handling personnel issues in M&As. While there are cases of HR people feeling optimistic about their role, there are also cases where HR was clearly marginalised during the process. Overall, we can characterise the HR role as taking one of three different forms.

First, and at one end of the spectrum, is the highly systematic, ordered approach to handling the post-merger restructuring. GlobalDrug, for example, went to great lengths to establish procedures for selecting people for posts in the merged company that would be perceived as fair, using outside consultants to enhance the feeling of objectivity, and moving quickly to harmonise terms and conditions. Those interviewed were very upbeat about how personnel issues had been handled in general and the role of HR in particular. A key factor here was the integration of HR with top management and the business divisions, and a number of respondents claimed that the role of HR was very influential. This was seen as stemming from the powerful role of HR in the dominant party to the merger, as well as the central role of the corporate HR director who is widely seen as the chief executive's right-hand man.

Second, an intermediate position would be where there is a limited role for HR but where the merger itself provided opportunities to promote the function. Perhaps the best example of this here is the case of Global FinServices, where the HR co-ordinator insisted that she be involved in discussions about integration. She repeatedly spoke to a general manager who, she reported, did not seem to want her involved, and yet by 'speaking his language' she managed to get involved in key meetings and to raise HR issues among the senior management team. In order to try to convince sceptical line and finance managers about the potential contribution of HR, she sought to emphasise in hard, quantitative terms the benefits of such involvement, and initially to concentrate on those aspects of HR for which others could see a direct bottom-line impact, such as pensions and share schemes.

Likewise in one of the utilities companies, an HR manager indicated that the French parent company was 'not used to HR playing a very proactive role', but that the importance of handling issues such as the merging of pension schemes had helped the function be seen in a more positive light. A similar story is evident at one of the oil companies, where HR had changed from 'the department that everyone hates' to a situation where one HR manager indicated that during the merger 'I suddenly felt that I had a real pivotal role in the organisation.' His account of the merger suggested that there was a realisation among managers in other functions that HR could make a key contribution in the areas of communicating with staff and in handling cultural integration.

Third, and at the opposite end of the spectrum, the management of people is more chaotic. The best instance of this was one of the IT companies, a specialist Anglo-American company that had grown rapidly through a string of acquisitions. Here, people in the acquired organisation were 'cherry-picked' on an opportunistic basis by business unit managers from the acquiring company, and 20 out of the 350 acquired employees brought grievance cases against

> '... earlier ... this research project ... revealed a concern amongst many HR managers that they had not been involved in the merger process at an early enough stage ...'

the company. It was clear that HR had been marginalised throughout the acquisition and were highly critical of the entire process: 'If you want to see how not to handle an acquisition, you've come to the right place.' The way in which decisions were taken with little or no HR involvement could arguably be linked to the problems that ensued; as well as the grievance cases mentioned above, the company was apparently in breach of TUPE regulations and was lucky to escape a series of tribunal cases.

An earlier stage of this research project, involving a survey of CIPD International Forum members (CIPD, 2000), had revealed a concern amongst many HR managers that they had not been involved in the merger process at an early enough stage and that they needed to get involved later to 'clear up the mess', as one put it. The case studies in this report all illustrate the importance of HR managers fighting their corner and pushing to raise HR issues on the senior management agenda. A more recent CIPD Forum meeting involved 20 members collectively sharing their senior management experience of merging or acquiring with well over 100 non-UK companies. Once again a key lesson expressed was the need for HR to be in a position of influence sufficiently early to influence outcomes, to make the case to the CEO for a presence on M&A teams, and to contribute fully to due diligence and integration processes (CIPD Guide, 2003). Where this is the case, the HR contribution to merger can be substantial, and the success of the integration for employees at all levels markedly improved.

In terms of the role of HR, you need to have a functional expert with change management experience ... HR must also be proactive and put their availability on record.

Some fairly simple due diligence ... just try and understand the culture and why they do this and why they do that, and why they are structured the way they are ... would save so much heartache.

When it came to the merger .... I suddenly felt I had a real pivotal role in the organisation ... HR was such an important aspect, at that stage about communication, about trying to support staff, about looking at what this means culturally for us even in the short term because at that stage you don't know if you're going to have a job any longer.

There is a greater credence given to the HR input ... The directors have seen what has gone on in the last two or three years and recognise the importance of strong HR processes, for example ... the importance of a strong selection process ... I wouldn't say they all appreciate it completely, but there is a recognition of the value of communication, internal communication, to the organisation which during these mergers was extremely important.

A lesson that I have learned from this is that the HR organisation has to very quickly stand up and stake out its role in this process. ... say 'this is what my role in strategy development ought to be' ... and actually to do that.

8 | Conclusions for management
Richard L Coates, Mercer Human Resource Consulting, September 2003

The research findings described in this report provide a very useful supplement to the experience of practitioners over a long period of time that M&As are fraught with difficulty. International M&As are even more problematical. In more cases than not, mergers result in a destruction of shareholder value, irreparable damage to organisations that were previously working satisfactorily and/or serious harm to the livelihood or careers of thousands of people. Despite this, M&As are still generally viewed as a legitimate business strategy by chief executives and boards, not to say venture capitalists.

Why do M&As fail and, perhaps more importantly, given their prevalence, what must be done to help them succeed? The research has some important lessons from organisations that have succeeded, as well as a few that have not.

The context of international M&As

Firstly, however, it is necessary to stress the variability of M&As. Writing in 2001, Joseph Bower of Harvard Business School described five different strategic rationales for mergers, and suggested that these would each fundamentally impact on the priorities for post-merger integration.[1] To give one example, a merger designed to consolidate an industry will have a very different primary driver (reducing headcount) than one aimed at geographic expansion or acquiring intellectual capital. This is echoed in Chapters 2 and 3 of this report.

Overlaying the different strategic rationales are other contextual variables which will also impact on either the content or the process of integration. Principally highlighted in this report are the effects of geography – acquiring cross-border operations, or acquiring an organisation with operations in many countries, compounds the problems. Legislative frameworks, ways of doing business and cultural differences will all provide hurdles not found to the same extent in single-country deals. This report comments on *home-country* and *host-country* effects – a useful addition to understanding the requirements of international M&As.

The nature of the industry will also affect integration needs as highlighted in some of the case studies. What is required in financial services or retail will be quite different from what is required in oil or utilities. For instance, the report shows how the handling of HR issues is quite different between the pharmaceuticals and the utilities sectors.

Impacting upon the process of integration are a number of other factors:

◻ the degree of openness between the parties pre-deal

◻ the regulatory frameworks that govern the merger

◻ the *rules of the road* – what terms have been agreed as part of the deal

◻ the degree of post-merger integration desired/required.

All these factors influence and complicate the process of acquisition, and organisations need to fully understand this contextual framework from the outset.

HR's Contribution to International Mergers and Acquisitions
Conclusions and summary

> '… cultural differences may have a huge impact on the outcome of a merger.'

Conclusion 1
Before embarking on acquisition, organisations must fully understand the strategic rationale underpinning it, together with the external constraints and opportunities for optimising success.

Organisations and culture

Usually ignored until too late in the process, cultural differences may have a huge impact on the outcome of a merger. This highlights the inadequacy of the due diligence process used by many organisations and the quality of pre-deal scenario planning that acquirers undertake.

Culture has organisational and national/regional dimensions that can be seen in a range of ways illustrated in the report. Many of these below are vitally important to how the business is run, some less so. All are emotive.

- decision-making processes (centralised or localised)
- formality/status or informality
- differing views of ethical behaviour (eg sales 'commissions' or kickbacks)
- open-plan or management offices
- dress code.

There are many more. What is clear from the research is that the nationality of the acquirer makes a significant difference to the style and culture of the new organisation. What is also clear is that most organisations do not research or understand the cultural issues or their likely impact on post-merger performance. This may be due to arrogance, ignorance, or simply being oblivious to the risks. In any case, the most likely effect of ignoring the cultural dimension, or riding roughshod over cherished cultural norms, will be disaffection and demotivation.

Conclusion 2
Ensure that cultural due diligence is carried out prior to a deal so that effective integration programmes can be implemented immediately post-deal.

As shown in Chapter 7, designing and populating a new organisation also has a significant impact on the success of the deal. A range of methods is described in the case studies, from arm-wrestling through 'picking up sides' to highly structured assessment-centre methodologies. Each has its drawbacks. Achieving balance at the expense of appointing the best person for every job will under-optimise the strength of the resultant team. Two people for every management role is obviously not a cost- and performance-effective solution. Long-winded assessment and selection processes, while overtly fair, may generate concern and stasis which undermines the benefits.

Conclusion 3
Move quickly but fairly in the appointment of new management teams at all levels in the business and deal humanely with the casualties.

Many mergers are predicated on 'achieving synergies', generally shorthand for reducing headcount. The case studies show that applying this in practice can vary widely from country to country because of local legislation or agreements and be far more time-consuming than anticipated. Internal politics and governmental pressure can

> 'A key issue ... is whether to harmonise terms and conditions, rewards and benefits.'

also play a part in undermining the strategy. Although the research does not contain conclusive evidence that the negotiations and compromises that occur during most post-merger periods directly affect the business performance, it is entirely plausible (even likely) that they do.

Conclusion 4
Identify realistic synergy targets. Deal-makers should be cautious in estimating both the timeframe and the potential cost of redundancies – over-optimism will lead to underperformance.

Contracts, rewards and benefits

A key issue in the integration phase is whether to harmonise terms and conditions, rewards and benefits. To do so is economically costly; not to do so may have a negative impact on morale. Various examples are given which illustrate the problem:

- balance between fixed and variable pay (status- or performance-driven)
- company cars (who is entitled, perceived value)
- share options
- pension schemes
- holiday entitlements.

This is an area where the goal may be clear – harmonisation – but the practice is very muddied. A number of the case-study participants have taken the 'pragmatic' view that differing arrangements can co-exist, and harmonisation can be reached over time. The constraints of TUPE (or equivalent), union agreements, and the potentially high costs mean that this is often the only practical solution.

The risk, again, is that it may be difficult to maintain morale and performance when similar jobs are rewarded differently. Further, the synergy savings predicted for the merger may be undermined by increased employment costs.

Conclusion 5
Ensure that due diligence provides comprehensive data on all aspects of reward and that the costs of harmonisation or 'pragmatism' are factored into the deal.

Making it happen

International M&As are highly complex and generate a plethora of things to be done, usually in a very short timeframe. Although there are only five or six mission-critical goals that will deliver the real value of the deal, there are 1,001 things that can erode it. Meanwhile business must continue as usual.

The key is highly effective project management, requiring

- dedicated resources (project teams, steering groups, external support)
- detailed allocated responsibilities
- risk identification, assessment and management
- problem-solving and quick-time escalation.

> 'Underpinning all of this ... is the need for frequent, targeted and personalised communication ...'

Project management does not have to be complicated to be effective, but poor project management will guarantee that the goals of the merger are not attained.

> **Conclusion 6**
> Establish early a flexible project management process and ensure that it has the necessary time, resources and processes to manage the transition.

Communication

Underpinning all of this process is the need for frequent, targeted and personalised communication to all interested parties, but particularly to employees. As described in Chapter 7, the ability to do this is sometimes compromised by the varying, and often conflicting, requirements of European or national legislation on employee consultation. In a number of the case studies, these made the task of communication more difficult, allowing progress only at the pace of the slowest. These complexities are rarely understood ahead of a deal, especially if the acquirer is from a country such as the USA, where there is no similar legislation.

However, communication should not only be conducted through formal channels of consultation. In an ideal world, there are a number of critical aspects to getting employee communication *right*:

- The general message must be clear, truthful and consistent (eg describing an acquisition as a 'merger of equals' is rarely the case, and can lead to compounding problems later).

- Senior management must be united in delivering the message – any hint of inconsistency will rapidly undermine the whole effort.

- All available media should be used – electronic, on paper and face-to-face – to ensure that all employees are reached.

- At all stages, employees should hear the message first from the company, not as all too frequently happens learning about an acquisition in the press or on television.

- Each employee has individual communication needs that must be addressed individually.

- Two-way communication is essential to engender buy-in and start the process of acceptance – contributing to solutions is the best way of building understanding and commitment.

Effective employee communication is a long-term and ongoing requirement in M&As. Never easy, especially with an international audience, it is an essential catalyst to accomplishing the necessary changes, and allowing the business to move on successfully. By contrast, inadequate communication – and the resultant loss of morale – will hasten the process of value-destruction.

> **Conclusion 7**
> Communicate, communicate, communicate – be consistent, truthful and timely.

The role of HR

Many of the critical issues which undermine the success of mergers are people-related, as has been amply illustrated by the report. Recent US research[2] has shown that where HR is more actively involved, mergers are more successful. This is particularly true with involvement at the strategic planning phase and in due diligence. The report also illustrates this point with the contrasting quotes from GlobalDrug and TeleCo.

It is clear why this should be. Early recognition and quantification of the costs and risks surrounding redundancies, creating new management structures, reward and cultural integration will undoubtedly better inform the deal-makers and make a head start on the integration planning process. Nevertheless, HR is often still a latecomer to the process, thrown the ball when the deal is done, and expected to deliver synergy targets which may turn out to be unrealistic. A recent CIPD Guide[3] describes in detail the role to which HR functions must aspire and the skills required to be effective.

Conclusion 8

HR must be integral to the M&A process from the outset. To achieve this, the function must be a credible business-partner and generate practical, financially astute and timely solutions.

In conclusion …

People as individuals and working together in teams are the essence of an organisation and ultimately what makes it effective. The quality, skills and motivation of people are what differentiate the good from the outstanding.

M&As focus primarily on the financial, economic and commercial aspects of the deal, and often only as an afterthought on people. Most senior executives recognise that people are their greatest asset, but just seem to overlook this mantra in the heat of a deal.

As this report illustrates so effectively, taking full account of the people issues in an M&A and managing them effectively will generate better short- and long-term results for employees, customers and shareholders alike.

Endnotes

1 Bower, Joseph (2001) 'Not all Mergers are Alike'. *Harvard Business Review*, March.

2 Schmidt, Jeffrey A. (ed.) (2002) *Making Mergers Work – The Strategic Importance of People*, USA, Society for Human Resource Management.

3 International Mergers and Acquisitions – the CIPD Guide to HR's Contribution to Success (2003), CIPD.

References

EUROPEAN FOUNDATION (2001)
'The Industrial Relations Implications of Mergers and Acquisitions'.
http://www.eiro.eurofound.ie/2001/02/study/index2.html

FAULKNER, D., PITKETHLY, R. AND CHILD, J. (2002)
'International Mergers and Acquisitions in the UK 1985–94:
A Comparison of National HRM Practices'. *International Journal of Human Resource Management*, Vol 13, No 1, pp106–122.

MERCER HUMAN RESOURCE CONSULTING (2002)
M&A – Leading Edge Approach to People Issues. London, Marsh & McLennan Companies.

PRICEWATERHOUSECOOPERS (2002)
The People Challenges of Corporate Transactions. London, PwC.

SCHULER, R., JACKSON, S. AND LUO, Y. (2003)
Managing Human Resources in Cross-Border Alliances. London, Routledge.

CIPD 2003
International Mergers and Acquisitions – a Guide.